Jennifer Brenton is a Criminal and Regulatory Barrister at 33 Bedford Row Chambers. She was called by Inner Temple in 2013 and, at the date of this book, has been in practice for just over 10 years. She spent an early part of her career seconded to a London Local Authority where she supervised the Prosecutions and Licensing Legal Department. From that experience, she developed a specialty in Regulatory and Licensing matters, alongside a general criminal practice.

Prior to prosecuting s82 EPA cases, she did a considerable number of cases defending landlords in Local Authority Prosecutions under the Houses in Multiple Occupation Regulations and the Selective Licensing Regime. When it comes to criminal proceedings for housing, she is experienced on both sides of the aisle.

As a criminal practitioner, her understanding is of the criminal courts and the criminal rules of evidence and procedure. As the Head of the EPA team at 33 Bedford Row Chambers and through providing seminars for solicitors and experts alike on different aspects of the EPA, she has learnt how to break this topic down in a way that can be readily understood.

A Practical Guide to Private Prosecutions Under Section 82 of the Environmental Protection Act 1990

A Practical Guide to Private Prosecutions Under Section 82 of the Environmental Protection Act 1990

Jennifer Brenton

Barrister, Inner Temple

MA (Hons)

Law Brief Publishing

Published 2024 by Law Brief Publishing, an imprint of Law Brief Publishing Ltd
30 The Parks
Minehead
Somerset
TA24 8BT

www.lawbriefpublishing.com

Paperback: 978-1-916698-05-5

PREFACE

This is, I hope, the book that I wish existed when I started prosecuting these cases.

This is an area which appears straightforward; a self-contained code in s82 and s79 Environmental Protection Act 1990 ("EPA"). It is intended to provide tenants with an efficient summary procedure to obtain legal redress when their property is not sufficiently safe for themselves and their families or is in such a state as to interfere with their quiet enjoyment of their home.

But things are not as straightforward as they appear.

Criminal proceedings without a criminal offence as such, present particular challenges.

The tenants (persons aggrieved) tend to be of limited means, living in social housing, local authority housing or other accommodation paid for through Universal Credit. The prosecutions are funded by way of Conditional Fee Agreements.

The Parties are often represented by firms and counsel who specialise in housing law, some of whom have more and some have less familiarity with criminal practice and procedure. Applications may be made for remedies which simply don't exist in the criminal courts. Every single issue and argument will often be taken.

In my experience the issues balloon far beyond what is reasonable. The "summary" procedure becomes protracted, and the costs escalate.

I hope that this book will assist practitioners on all sides to better understand this topic. So that maybe, in a Magistrates' Court somewhere, a s82 EPA case can be dealt with in the way that the legislation intended; efficiently, summarily and providing the speedy redress that is its purpose.

Scope of this Book

The number of these cases is rising. This may be due to the cost of living crisis, it may be due to the pressures on Local Authorities and Housing providers, it may simply be that they are being contested more often than they were previously. I do not know. But, as these cases rise, so do the reported decisions of the Higher Courts. The law in this book is up to date at the 31st of May 2024. I am aware of at least one pending appeal (keep an eye on CFAs), but I am sure that there are more.

I find with these cases that every day is a school day. What I have included here is, in summary, the law that I know on the main issues as well as practical advice from my experience. It is, by no means, comprehensive. But I hope that it will provide a jumping-off point for most of the problems that you may encounter under s82 EPA.

Acknowledgements

With thanks to Jonathan Morkill, for taking a chance on me on my first of these cases and bearing with me ever since.

With thanks to my clerks, for supporting my EPA endeavours.

With thanks to my pupil, Nina Reinach, for spending a sunny Sunday afternoon digging through Hansard and learning about CFAs.

With thanks to my partner, Robert Fitt, for listening (or pretending to listen) to my endless musings on mice and mould.

And finally with thanks to Law Brief Publishing, for allowing me to write this book and for the infinite patience awaiting its delivery.

Without you all, this book would not have been possible.

Jennifer Brenton
June 2024

CONTENTS

CHAPTER ONE

INTRODUCTION

1.1 What is s82 Environmental Protection Act 1990?

S82 EPA provides a mechanism by which a tenant ("person aggrieved") may take their landlord ("person responsible") to the Magistrates' Court seeking an order compelling them to take specified action to abate a nuisance arising from the state of their property(s82(2)) with criminal sanctions if they fail to comply, as well as requiring them to pay the costs of the proceedings (s82(12)).

It is intended to be an efficient summary procedure by which tenants can obtain speedy legal redress where their property is not safe or is in such a state as to undermine their use and enjoyment. A legal code encapsulated in s82 and s79 EPA.

1.2 Criminal Proceedings without a Crime: The Legal Fiction

A s82 EPA case is a criminal prosecution. The Prosecution bear the burden to prove the case to the criminal standard (so that the court is sure).

What makes s82 unusual in the run of criminal proceedings is that there has not actually been any criminal offence when the matter comes to court.

It could, on a comparison with s80 EPA (Local Authority powers and Abatement Notices), be suggested that the "offence" arises when the Defendant has failed to comply with the Abatement Notice. This is the earliest date from which compensation can be calculated (see **R v Liverpool Crown Court ex p Cooke** [1997] 1 WLR 700).

It could be argued that the offence only arises if the nuisance has not been abated by the date of the hearing, as it is only in these circumstances that the court may impose a fine and order the Defendant to pay compensation (see s82(2)) and **R v Dudley Magistrates' Court** [1999] 1 W.L.R 642)

It was suggested in Parliament, when considering amending the Courts and Legal Services Act 1990 to allow for Conditional Fee Agreements ("CFAs") in s82 cases, that these cases were more akin to civil injunctions. This proposition formed a tenet of the argument; CFAs should be allowed to fund s82 cases as Legal Aid would be available to impecunious claimants in such civil cases.

Whatever the closest comparator, the fact that s82 cases are criminal cases without a crime presents certain challenges. These must be understood for any prosecution or defence to be effective.

CHAPTER TWO

WHAT IS A STATUTORY NUISANCE?

"Statutory Nuisance" is defined in s79 EPA. This is a definition which applies equally to Local Authority Abatement Notices (under s80 EPA) and private prosecutions for Abatement Orders under s82 EPA. It is therefore a more far-reaching definition than is likely to be used for s82 EPA prosecutions including, eg. under s72(1)(g) EPA a definition of noise nuisance.

For the purposes of s82 EPA the almost exclusive definition is s79(1)(a):

> *Any premises in such a state as to be prejudicial to health or a nuisance*

It must be proven that the state of the premises is such as to be:

1. Prejudicial to health; **or**

2. A nuisance

2.1 "Prejudicial to Health"

"Prejudicial to health" is defined in s79(7) EPA: means injurious or likely to cause injury to health. In order to prove that the state of the premises is injurious or likely to cause injury to health, expert evidence is required (please see Ch 8) but medical evidence is not.

O'Toole v Knowsley MBC (2000) 32 H.L.R 420

The decision of the Magistrates' Court to dismiss an application under s82 EPA as the Complainant had not adduced medical evidence of the effect of the mould/damp on herself or her children was quashed by the High Court. The evidence of the expert as to how the state of the premises was prejudicial to health was sufficient and the Justices were not entitled to reject it due to the absence of medical evidence in support.

2.2 "Or a Nuisance"

The term "nuisance" is not defined in the Act or in any citing caselaw. It is unfortunately circular that the definition of nuisance under s79(1)(a) can come down to a "statutory nuisance is a nuisance".

The term should be given its natural meaning. The generally accepted definition adopted by experts and the courts is substantial or unreasonable interference with the Complainant's use and enjoyment of the property.

If relying on this part of the definition, the most pertinent evidence is likely to come from the Complainant as to the effect of the nuisance. For example, regularly seeing mice in the kitchen, cleaning mouse droppings continuously, disposing of dead mice, lack of sleep and/or anxiety related to the mice presence, children refusing to go into parts of the house etc.

It should be noted that, although not required by the Act, the courts tend to import an objective element to this definition, ie. what would a reasonable person be expected to tolerate? Whilst one individual might find a small patch of damp in their bathroom irritating and unsightly it would be unlikely that the court would accept that this was enough to amount to substantial interference with a reasonable person's use and enjoyment of the property. However, if there were widespread black mould all over the sole family bathroom, this would be far more likely to reach the objectivity threshold.

Even if relying on this limb, expert evidence will still be required to establish that the nuisance arose due to the state of the premises and that the Defendant is the "person responsible" (see Ch 3.2).

CHAPTER THREE

THE PERSON AGGRIEVED & THE PERSON RESPONSIBLE (OR OWNER)

3.1 Who may bring Proceedings under s82 EPA? "The Person Aggrieved"

S82(1) *A magistrates' court may act under this section on a complaint … made by any person on the ground that he is aggrieved by the existence of a statutory nuisance.*

"Person aggrieved" is not legally defined in the Act but is understood to mean a person who is adversely affected by the nuisance. For cases brought under s82 EPA this generally means the tenant of the property which is affected by the nuisance.

Although these cases are usually brought by the tenant, "person aggrieved" could also cover other inhabitants of the property or sub-tenants as each are adversely affected by the nuisance. The existence of a contractual relationship with the Defendant is not required by the Act but may have bearing on establishing whether the Defendant is the "person responsible" (see Ch 3.2).

In the unusual case of **Watkins v Aged Merchant Seamen's Homes [2018] EWHC 2410 (Admin)**, the High Court considered the definition of "person aggrieved". This case involved a s82 EPA prosecution brought by a Complainant who was initially occupying the premises under a licence, but by the time that the prosecution was initiated, that licence had been terminated by a Notice to Quit and she had remained in occupation without paying rent. By the date of the trial, a possession order had been made by the County Court against the Complainant but the Complainant remained in occupation. The Magistrates dismissed the information on the basis that the Complainant did not have standing to bring the prosecution. This was overturned on appeal. The High Court found that whether the Complainant was a "person aggrieved" was to be determined at the date of complaint. It was a question of fact and degree. A Complainant in actual occupation of the premises (at the date of the complaint) would be a person aggrieved, even if that occupation was deemed unlawful.

Another important point which arises from this case is that if the Complainant is a "person aggrieved" at the date of the making of the complaint under s82(1), they do not then lose that standing if they are evicted or cease to reside in the property before the court comes to consider an Abatement Order under s82(2) (see Ch 4). That order does not require proof that the Complainant remains "a person aggrieved" at the date of the hearing, their standing is established conclusively at the date of complaint. In the Judgment of Kerr J, at para 44; "*I have no difficulty with the proposition that though her victory may be pyrrhic as regards her personal interests, the complaints can survive and enure for the benefit of subsequent occupiers or the public.*"

3.2 Who to Prosecute? "The Person Responsible"

S82(4) sets out who proceedings under s82 should be brought against:

> *(4) Proceedings for an order under subsection (2) above shall be brought—*
>
> > *(a) except in a case falling within paragraph (b), (c) or (d) below, against the person responsible for the nuisance;*
> >
> > *(b) where the nuisance arises from any defect of a structural character, against the owner of the premises;*
> >
> > *(c) where the person responsible for the nuisance cannot be found, against the owner or occupier of the premises.*

3.2.1 Who is the "person responsible for the nuisance" (s82(4)(a))?

"Person responsible" is defined in s79(7):

> *In relation to statutory nuisance, means the person to whose act, default or sufferance the nuisance is attributable.*

The Landlord is usually the Defendant as the "person responsible" for the nuisance. This may be down to the specific terms of the lease as to their repairing obligations but, even in the absence of a copy of the lease (as is often the case) or where the lease is silent on the issue, s11 Landlord and Tenant Act 1985 ("LTA") can be relied upon.

S11(1) LTA implies the following term into the lease agreement:

> *(1) In a lease to which this section applies … there is implied a covenant by the lessor—*
>
> > *(a) to keep in repair the structure and exterior of the dwelling-house (including drains, gutters and external pipes),*
> >
> > *(b) to keep in repair and proper working order the installations in the dwelling-house for the supply of water, gas and electricity and for sanitation (including basins, sinks, baths and sanitary conveniences, but not other fixtures, fittings and appliances for making use of the supply of water, gas or electricity), and*
> >
> > *(c) to keep in repair and proper working order the installations in the dwelling-house for space heating and heating water.*

For example, in the case of a nuisance arising from the presence of mice, the Landlord would likely be in breach of s11(1)(a) LTA; the duty to keep in repair the structure and exterior of the dwelling house. In properties with no structural disrepair (and bearing in mind mice can enter through holes as small as 5mm), it would be unlikely that a sufficient number of mice could enter the property so as to take residence, multiply and cause an ongoing statutory nuisance. This is a point which may be accepted by the court by way of judicial notice but must also be addressed in the expert report.

It may (and sometimes is) suggested that open windows or ajar doors can cause a mouse infestation. To which the answer is quite simple – most homes open their windows and open their doors, but do not suffer from mouse infestation.

If mice are entering the property, it is likely that the landlord has failed to "*keep in repair the structure and exterior of the dwelling-house*". The breach of this repairing obligation would be a "default" (under s79(7) EPA) to which the nuisance is attributable.

3.2.2 "Structure and exterior of the dwelling house"

In the case of **Irvine's Estate v Moran [1990] 5 WLUK 203**, the High Court considered the definition of "structure and exterior of the dwelling house" under s32 Housing Act 1961 (now s11 LTA)

Mr Recorder Thayne Forbes QC delivered the Judgment for the Court of Appeal in this case. At p.5 of that judgment, he states:

> *The structure of the dwellinghouse is something less than the overall dwellinghouse itself. Of course, the difficulty that is posed is deciding to what more limited aspects of the overall dwellinghouse the word "structure" is addressed. I have come to the view that the structure of the dwellinghouse consists of those elements of the overall dwellinghouse which give it its essential appearance, stability and shape. The expression does not extend to the many and various ways in which the dwellinghouse will be fitted out, equipped, decorated and generally made to be habitable.*

At p.6 of the judgment he directly addresses the issue of whether windows and doors would fall within the definition of the "structure of the dwellinghouse":

> *Windows pose a slightly different problem. I have some hesitation about this, but bearing in mind that one is talking about a dwellinghouse, and rejecting as I do the suggestion that one should use "load-bearing" as the only touchstone to determining what is the structure of the dwellinghouse in its essential material elements, I have come to the conclusion that*

> *windows do form part of the structure of the dwellinghouse. My conclusion might be different if one were talking about windows in, let us say, an agricultural building. The essential material elements may change, depending on the nature and use of the building in question. In the case of a dwellinghouse, it seems to me that an essential and material element in a dwellinghouse, using ordinary common sense and an application of the words "structure of the dwellinghouse" without limiting them to a concept such as "load-bearing", must include the external windows and doors.*

This judgment is essentially repeated in the '**Housing Health and Safety Rating System, Operating Guidance**' (issued by the Government under the Housing Act 2004). This Guidance is used by Environmental Health Officers to evaluate premises for Local Authorities to determine whether the premises are safe for habitation and make any emergency orders if they are not.

At p.38, Annex A, para A6 it states:

> *The words "exterior and structural elements of the dwelling" are not limited to the loadbearing elements, but include all those elements which give a dwelling its essential appearance, stability and shape, and those which provide protection from the climate. It includes, for example, means of access, amenity space, foundations, walls (including internal plasterwork), roof, windows, doors, and ceilings. While it includes protective finishes (including paintwork to timber), it does not normally include the internal surface decoration such as wallpaper and emulsion paint.*

3.2.3 When is the Defendant no longer the "person responsible"?

In order for the Landlord to comply with their repairing obligations, they must be aware that there is an issue with disrepair. A landlord will not be in breach of the express or implied terms of the tenancy agreement if the tenant has not informed them that there is an issue.

Equally, if the tenant has informed them that there is an issue, but then wilfully or unreasonably obstructs their efforts to repair, the landlord may no longer be the person responsible. The question is whether the Landlord has done all that is reasonable to gain entry to effect repairs. This is an evaluative decision for the court to determine based on the evidence, and the court may take into account efforts made by the Landlord prior to the service of the abatement notice (see **Taylor v Burton [2021] EWHC 1454 (Admin)** following **Jones v Walsall MBC [2002] EWHC 1232 (Admin)**).

From a practical perspective, it should be noted that the repairs required to effectively abate nuisance by mice presence or by damp and mould are not limited to one or two visits from appropriately qualified repairmen. In the case of mice, there needs to be a course of proofing and baiting works in order to first exterminate the mice and then block all entry points to ensure that they do not return. This is a process which, depending on the extent of the mice activity, can take many months of regular visits; emptying traps, relaying bait and poison, proofing old entry points and new ones as they arise.

It is likely that during this process, appointments will be missed. This can be due to the landlord or pest control failing to notify the tenant in good time of the need for access, the tenant missing the letter notifying or simply forgetting the appointment. Where there has been a wholesale failure by the Tenant to provide any access despite the landlord making all reasonable efforts, it is likely that the Defendant will no longer be considered the "person responsible". However, where there have been a handful of (accidentally) missed appointments in a long course of repair works, where access has otherwise been regularly and willingly given, this is unlikely to shift the responsibility from the Landlord to the Tenant. It is a question of fact and degree for the court to determine on all of the evidence.

See also: **Warner v LBC [1984] 3 WLUK 171** and **Carr v Hackney LBC [1995] 2WLUK 344.**

As a practical point, it is strongly advised that the Abatement Notice (addressed at Ch 5.1) contains clear instructions to the Defendant to contact the prosecuting solicitors if there are any issues accessing the property, with a statement confirming that the prosecuting firm will assist to ensure that reasonable access is given and to ensure that appointments are not missed. If the Defendant does not take this step, this will assist the prosecution to rebut any suggestion that the Defendant is no longer the person responsible due to the Complainant missing appointments.

3.3 Who to Prosecute? The "Owner"

3.3.1 What is a "Defect of a Structural Character"?

This issue only arises where the landlord is separate from the "owner" of the property.

S82(4)(b) provides that where nuisance arises due to a "defect of structural character", the proceedings must be brought against the "owner" of the premises. This is to be distinguished from s82(4)(a) (proceedings against the person responsible) which only applies *if* s82(4)(b) does not.

The EPA does not provide a definition of "structural defect" but, following the above, it must be something different from the Landlord's obligation to keep in repair "the structure and exterior of the dwelling house".

This is a problem which the courts have been grappling with and, at times, coming to irreconcilably different conclusions.

It is suggested that the difference between:

a. a case which should be brought against the Landlord under s82(4)(a) as the person responsible due to breach of their obligation to keep in repair "the structure and exterior of the dwelling"; and

b. a case which should be brought against the "Owner" under s82(4)(b) as the nuisance arises from a "defect of a structural character"

is to be found in the definition of the word "defect".

It is suggested that the distinction cannot be explained by the definition of the word "structural" as this appears in both s82(4)(a) (by virtue of the Landlord's duty under s11(1)(a) LTA) and in s82(4)(b).

The Upper Tribunal (Lands Chamber) considered this distinction in the case of **City of London Corp v Various Leaseholders of Great Arthur House [2019] UKUT 341 (LT)**. The issue was to distinguish (for the purposes of the service charge) between repairing costs for keeping in repair the "structure and exterior of the dwelling" versus repairing costs due to a "structural defect". The former costs were rechargeable to the tenants under the long leasehold agreement, the latter costs were to be paid only by the Local Authority owner and were not rechargeable to the tenants.

LTA which would be a "default or sufferance" to which the nuisance is attributable. One without the other would not by itself cause the nuisance, but together the nuisance arose.

3.3.3 Who is the "owner" of the Premises?

The High Court considered the definition of "owner" for the purposes of s80(2))(b) EPA (which mirrors s82(4)(b)) in the case of **Camden London Borough Council v Gunby [2000] 1 W.L.R. 465 (1999).** The Council served an Abatement Notice on a firm of surveyors who acted as managing agents for the property (and collected the rent), alleging nuisance arising from a structural defect. The Managing agents appealed, claiming that the notice should have been served on the freehold owners of the property. The High Court interpreted the term "owner" by recourse to the legislative history. The Court concluded that "owner" meant:

> *The person for the time being receiving the rackrent of the premises in connection with which the word was used, whether on his own account or as agent or trustee for any other person*

The appeal was accordingly dismissed.

Whilst the case of **Gunby** is unclear as to whether this definition would exclude the actual owner (ie. the legal owner on the Land Registry) where they do not receive the rack rent, it is clear that landlords would be considered "owners" for the purposes of s82(4)(b) even when they do not legally own the property. The focus must be on who is paid the rack rent.

3.4 "Person Responsible" v "Owner": A Distinction without a Difference?

The law has therefore come to a position where, if there is structural disrepair leading to the nuisance, the landlord is likely to be the correct defendant under s82(4)(a) as the "person responsible" due to s11 LTA. Equally if there is a structural defect leading to the nuisance, the landlord is likely to be the correct defendant under s82(4)(b) as the person receiving the rack rent, whether on his own account or as agent for another.

This may solve a practical issue. It will be very difficult for Environmental Health Practitioners (who tend to act as Experts in these cases) to determine where there are structural issues, whether these are "defects" (ie. issues in the design, construction or modification of the building) or whether these arise from a failure to keep the structure and exterior in repair. This problem can be avoided as, in either event, the person receiving the rack rent will likely be the correct defendant.

CHAPTER FOUR

TWO POINTS IN TIME: S82(2) V S82(12)

Given the delay between the making of the complaint (laying the information) and the matter coming to court for trial or plea, it is not unusual for significant remedial work to have taken place between. This often means that the nuisance has been abated by the time that the matter comes to court for determination.

However, that is not the end of the case. If the nuisance has been abated by the date of the court hearing and is not likely to recur, the Prosecution will no longer seek an abatement order under <u>s82(2)</u> but will nonetheless be entitled to a costs order under <u>s82(12)</u> if the nuisance was in existence at the date of the complaint.

This has legal implications in terms of what must be proven depending on what is being sought, and practical implications in terms of the timing of evidence to ensure it is most contemporaneous to the key dates for proof.

4.1 Seeking an Abatement Order under S82(2): Nuisance in existence or likely to recur <u>now</u>

<u>S82(2) EPA</u>

> *If the magistrates' court … is satisfied that the alleged nuisance exists, or that although abated it is likely to recur on*

4.2 Seeking a Costs Order under S82(12): Nuisance in existence at the date of the complaint

S82(12) EPA

> *Where on the hearing of proceedings for an order under subsection (2) above it is proved that the alleged nuisance existed at the date of the making of the complaint … then, whether or not at the date of the hearing it still exists or is likely to recur, the court … shall order the defendant … in such proportions as appears fair and reasonable to pay to the person bringing the proceedings such amount as the court… considers reasonably sufficient to compensate him for any expenses properly incurred by him in the proceedings*

For the Court to make a Costs Order against the Defendant, the Prosecution must prove to the criminal standard that:

1. The Nuisance was in existence at the date of the complaint; and

2. The Defendant was the "person responsible" and/or the nuisance arose from a "defect of a structural character" and the Defendant was the "owner".

It should be noted that unlike s82(2), s82(12) does not include circumstances where the nuisance was abated but "likely to recur". The Prosecution must prove that, at the date of the information, the nuisance was in existence, ie. the state of the premises was such as to be prejudicial to health or a nuisance.

The date of complaint will be established by documentary evidence of when the information was laid and received by the court. This is usually done by producing the emails containing the information and accompanying documents (this is addressed at Ch 5.2) between the court and the Prosecuting Firm.

Similarly to s82(2) applications, the Prosecution must provide contemporaneous evidence to the date of the complaint of the existence of the nuisance. An Expert inspection must take place as shortly as practicable before the complaint is laid.

As with s82(2) applications, if there is a delay between the inspection and laying the information in which the Defence can show that remedial works were undertaken, this may be fatal to an application under s82(12) (depending on the other evidence) if the Prosecution cannot therefore make the court sure of the state of the premises at the date of complaint.

4.3 Abatement Orders & Costs Orders: Statutory Duty not Discretion

Both s82(2) and s82(12) contain statutory duties. If the Prosecution have proven the elements set out above, the court **shall** make the order.

However, both Abatement Orders and Costs Orders do require the courts to make an evaluative judgment. In determining the terms of the Abatement Order, the court must evaluate the evidence available as to what is necessary and likely to be effective to abate the nuisance or prevent its recurrence, with due consideration to practicality, cost and the likely length of time to carry out the work effectively. Equally in making a Costs Order, the court needs to assess what expenses (costs) were "properly incurred", what amount is "reasonably sufficient" to compensate for those expenses and, where there are multiple defendants, what is a "fair and reasonable proportion" that each should be ordered to pay (this is addressed in Ch 8).

CHAPTER FIVE

COMMENCING PROCEEDINGS

5.1 The Abatement Notice

Before an information may be laid at the Magistrates' court under s82 EPA, the Complainant must first serve an "Abatement Notice" (often also referred to as a "notice of intended prosecution (NIP)") in accordance with s82(6)-(7).

S82(6)-(7) EPA:

> *(6) The person aggrieved by the nuisance shall give to that person such notice in writing of his intention to bring the proceedings as is applicable to proceedings in respect of a nuisance of that description and the notice shall specify the matter complained of.*
>
> *(7) The notice of the bringing of proceedings in respect of a statutory nuisance required by subsection (6) above which is applicable is—*
>
> > *(a) …*
> >
> > *(b) in the case of a nuisance of any other description, not less than twenty-one days' notice;*

The Abatement Notice must:

1. Specify "the matter complained of"

2. Provide not less than 21 days from date of service for the Defendant to abate the nuisance.

5.1.1 "The Matter Complained Of"

Generally this follows the wording of s79(1)(a), eg. "The state of the premises is such as to be prejudicial to health or a nuisance". The Notice should then specify the form of the nuisance, eg. Mould and damp or Rodent/Mouse presence

Any prosecution following the Abatement Notice can only be based on the alleged nuisance in the Abatement Notice. If, for example the Abatement Notice alleges a nuisance by rodent/mouse presence and the Expert then finds there is also an actionable nuisance by damp and mould, that could not form part of the complaint unless and until another abatement notice had been served and not complied with.

The Notice must then state why the Defendant is responsible, eg.

- "The Defendant is the person responsible as the landlord of the premises"; or
- "The nuisance arises from defects of a structural character and the Defendant is the owner of the property"; or
- (if both) the defendant is the person responsible as the landlord of the premises and/or the nuisance arises from defects of a structural character and the defendant is the owner of the property.

Pearshouse v Birmingham City Council [1999] Env L.R 536

The Magistrates' Court dismissed an information on the basis that the Abatement Notice did not contain sufficient detail or set out the steps to be taken to abate the nuisance. The High Court quashed the decision.

The procedure under s82 EPA was intended to be a simple procedure to enable a citizen to obtain redress. The Abatement Notice should contain such detail as was reasonable in all the circumstances to enable the Recipient to make any necessary inspection and then take practical steps to eliminate the nuisance. It would frustrate Parliament's intention to require unnecessary technicality.

5.1.2 21 Days to Abate

The Notice must specify the period of time to abate the nuisance, which must be no less than 21 days from the date that the notice is served.

The date of service is usually established by the signature of the recipient on the date that the notice was received. For this reason (even though not required by the Act) it is important that Abatement Notices are served by registered and signed for post, such that a signature with a date will be provided to the prosecuting firm upon receipt by the Defendant.

R v Dudley Magistrates' Court [1999] 1 W.L.R 642

The Complainant served an abatement notice providing 21 days to abate the nuisance. The Defendant acted promptly and drew up a list of works to be completed, but these could not be done within 21 days. The Complainant laid an information at the Magistrates' Court shortly after the expiration of the Notice. The Magistrates granted the Defendant an adjournment of 9 weeks and did not take a plea. When the matter returned to court, the nuisance had been abated. The Magistrates dismissed the complaint and declined to make a costs order under s82(12) EPA.

The High Court quashed the decision. S82(6)-(7) simply requires the service of a notice and 21 days to be allowed for abatement, whether that can be affected within that time is irrelevant (in most cases it will not be possible). The Complainant is entitled after the expiration of 21 days to lay an information and, if the nuisance is ongoing on that date, the court shall make a costs order in favour of the Complainant under s82(12).

5.2 The Complaint (Information)

5.2.1 "Complaint" means Information

s50 Magistrates' Courts Act 1980: Construction of references to complaint in enactments dealing with offences:

> *In any enactment conferring power on a magistrates' court to deal with an offence, or to issue a summons or warrant against a person suspected of an offence, on the complaint of any person, for references to a complaint there shall be substituted references to an information.*

References in the EPA to making a complaint or to the date of complaint refer to the laying of the information.

5.2.2 What must the information contain?

The prosecution is commenced by laying the information at the Magistrates' court and requesting a summons for the Defendant (s1 MCA). The Criminal Procedure Rules 2020, Part 7 "Starting a Prosecution in a Magistrates' Court" apply.

CrimPR 7.2 – 7.3 requires that an Information must:

- Contain details of the offence,
- Identify the legislation that created the offence,
- Give details of the alleged defendant,
- Give details of the applicant or informant.

Obviously with prosecutions under s82 there has not been an "offence" as such. The information should set out (in similar terms to the Abatement Notice) the nature of the nuisance, why the Defendant is the person responsible, the address of the premises, the relevant section of the EPA and provide the necessary information for contacting the Defendant and the Complainant.

Generally, the information should be accompanied by a statement from the Complainant which contains specifics of the alleged nuisance and a "Certificate of Outcome of Inspection" or report from an Expert, which certifies that the state of the premises is such as to be prejudicial to health or a nuisance. A copy of the Abatement Notice and proof of service may also be included.

5.2.3 What is a "Certificate of Outcome of Inspection"?

The 'Certificate of Outcome of Inspection' is a document provided by the Prosecution Expert upon inspecting the property which certifies that:

a. They are duly qualified expert and they are aware of their obligations to the court

b. They have inspected the premises on X date,

c. The state of the premises is such as to be prejudicial to health or a nuisance,

d. The nature of that nuisance, and

e. The Defendant is the person responsible as the nuisance arises from, eg. Failure to keep the structure and exterior of the property in repair.

A 'Certificate of Outcome of Inspection' is similar to, eg. a Streamlined forensics report. It is not a complete report, but it is a certified document from a duly qualified individual stating what their opinion will be. These are often used in EPA cases because of the urgency of the information being laid as soon as possible after the inspection (see Ch 4).

A 'Certificate of Outcome of Inspection' does not replace a report. A report from the Expert should follow and be served on the Defendant with the summons and accompanying documentation or, if not yet available, by the date of the First Appearance.

5.3 The First Appearance

The Defendant must be asked to enter a "plea" to the Summons. This generally will be "Guilty" or "Not Guilty" but they may equally be asked whether they accept or reject the allegations. CrimPR Rule 3.16 sets out the procedure to be followed.

It is desirable for trials to be listed in front of a District Judge due to the requirement of expert evidence, the (likely) voluminous papers and the complexity of the case.

5.3.1 Service of Defence Evidence

The usual rules regarding service of the Prosecution case and disclosure apply to s82 prosecutions. This means that there is no legal requirement for the Defence to provide the Prosecution or the Court with their evidence or witness statements, other than to provide the information required by the 'Preparation for Effective Trial' form and comply with the Standard Directions.

However, the courts have extensive inherent case management powers beyond the rules contained in the Criminal Procedure and Investigations Act 1996 ("CPIA").

CrimPR Rule 3

By CrimPR Rule 3.2, the Court is under a duty to further the overriding objective by active case management.

> *(1) The court must further the overriding objective by actively managing the case.*
>
> *(2) Active case management includes—*
>
> > *(a) the early identification of the real issues;*
> >
> > *(b) the early identification of the needs of witnesses;*
> >
> > *(c) achieving certainty as to what must be done, by whom, and when, in particular by the early setting of a timetable for the progress of the case;*
> >
> > *(d) monitoring the progress of the case and compliance with directions;*
> >
> > *(e) ensuring that evidence, whether disputed or not, is presented in the shortest and clearest way;*
> >
> > *(f) discouraging delay, dealing with as many aspects of the case as possible on the same occasion, and avoiding unnecessary hearings;*
> >
> > *(g) encouraging the participants to co-operate in the progression of the case; and*
> >
> > *(h) making use of technology.*

By CrimPR Rule 3.5, in fulfilling its duty under Rule 3.2 the court may give any direction or take any step to actively manage the case (unless inconsistent with legislation).

In addressing case management directions at the First Appearance on a s82 prosecution it is important that the court has this duty and this power at the forefront of its mind. In general (and often it is agreed), directions should be given for service of the full defence case – all witness statements and documents to be relied upon, usually sequential to service of the prosecution case.

There are many reasons why this approach should be followed in s82 cases (whereas in most criminal cases it would not be required):

- The centrality of expert evidence – they need a clear view of the issues and evidence of both sides to provide a properly informed opinion;

- The complexity of the issues – there are numerous legal issues which tend to arise in these cases, without proper notice of the issue and the grounds for the argument a trial may be stalled as an ambush;

- The number of documents – the Defence are likely to produce significant documentation detailing the history of the tenancy (where asserting they are not the person responsible) and the steps taken to address the nuisance, eg. Pest control reports spanning months.

5.3.2 Legal Arguments: Standard Trial Preparation Time Limits

In addition, attention should be paid by advocates to the 'Standard trial preparation time limits' which are summarised at p.9 of the 'Preparation for Effective Trial Form' (January 2023 version) ("PET form"). Particularly paras d-e regarding Disclosure Applications and paras w-x regarding Points of Law including Abuse of Process.

If there is likely to be a legal argument regarding abuse of process, an application to exclude evidence or issues to be taken with disclosure, these should be identified at the First Appearance, noted in the PET form and directions should be made. In the absence of Directions, the parties must comply with the time-limits set out in the CrimPR.

5.3.3 Case Management Directions: Matters to Consider

The Prosecutor should bring to the court proposed case management directions and the parties should then endeavour to agree the directions before the hearing. The court will not be bound by the proposed directions but is likely to be guided by the parties agreement.

S82 Prosecutions are not standard criminal cases and, as a result, the standard criminal directions given by the Magistrates' Court at typical First Appearances will not be sufficient. Practical thought must be given to the sequencing and timing of the directions.

First (as is standard) the Prosecution must serve their case (including their first Expert Report) and primary disclosure.

If the Defence are to be required to serve their case, they should know clearly the case they have to meet before being required to do so. If the Defence are intending to rely on an Expert, service of their case should include their first Expert Report or, if impracticable, their Expert Report should follow shortly after.

If there are likely to be issues with disclosure, consideration must be given as to whether the disputed disclosure is likely to include material which may affect the expert's opinion. If it will, the directions must ensure that the disclosure issues are resolved and any disclosure provided prior to the Expert Report.

Where there are to be opposing Experts, there must be a joint meeting (and ideally joint inspection) followed by a joint report or summary of the issues agreed and in dispute between the experts (see Ch 6).

If there are to be legal arguments, there must be directions for service of skeleton arguments and consideration should be given to whether the arguments require resolution at a hearing prior to the trial date or whether they can be resolved at the outset of the trial. If the latter, additional time estimates should be provided to ensure that the case can still be accommodated within the allocated window.

The most likely legal arguments will be abuse of process or applications to exclude evidence, such as expert evidence. It is strongly recommended, particularly for applications to exclude expert evidence, that this is dealt with at a Further Case Management Hearing prior to the trial. If the Defence take issue with the admissibility of the Prosecution Expert's evidence and the court agrees this is likely to be fatal to the Prosecution case unless there is still time for the Prosecution to instruct an alternative expert prior to the trial. This is almost as important for an issue over the admissibility of a Defence Expert, without that evidence the Defence will find it very difficult, if not impossible, to properly challenge the Prosecution case.

Consideration should also be given to the points set out at Chapter 4 (Two Points in Time: s82(2) v s82(12)). If the Prosecution will be seeking an Abatement Order at trial, there will need to be updated and contemporaneous evidence of the state of the property at the date of trial. This will involve a further statement from the Complainant and a further inspection by, at least, the Prosecution Expert and, ideally, jointly by both experts.

5.3.4 Failure to Comply with Court Directions

Unlike in civil proceedings, failure to comply with the CrimPR or court's directions does not have any automatic consequences. If a party fails, eg. To serve their expert report in time, that does not automatically render that report inadmissible.

The criminal courts have no power to strike out prosecutions or issue a summary or default judgment for failure to comply with directions. The Magistrates' court has no power to dismiss the case. A prosecution under s82 ends only in one of the following ways:

1. Acceptance by the Defence (ie. Guilty plea) with the orders that follow;
2. Court determination of the evidence and
    a. conclusion that the case is proven with the orders that follow; or
    b. conclusion that the case is not proven with the summons then dismissed
3. Stay of proceedings as an abuse of process; or
4. Withdrawal of the summons.

Although there are no automatic consequences, failure to comply with the court's directions without proper explanation and notice is likely to have adverse consequences. As set out at Ch 5.3.1 the court has a duty to further the overriding objective by active case management and, to put that duty into effect, the court has extensive inherent case management powers.

The parties are under an obligation to cooperate with each other. If one party has an issue complying with a court direction with a proper explanation and this can be resolved without affecting the trial date, the parties are expected to cooperate and to agree alternative directions. If it is not possible for the parties to agree, or if the breach of the direction will inevitably affect the trial date, the "breaching" party should apply to the court at the earliest opportunity for the matter to be listed for case management.

Adjournments are not granted by the Magistrates' courts as a matter of course. There is a strong emphasis on "speedy summary justice", adjournments are to be the exception and not the rule. Where adjournments must be sought, it must be done in a timely manner with full and proper explanation. Adjournment applications on the day of trial are far less likely to be successful and, even if they do succeed, may well end up with adverse costs orders.

- informs the court if their opinion changes.

CrimPR Rule 19.3 sets out the procedure for introduction of expert evidence.

6.1 What the Report must Contain

CrimPR Rule 19.4 sets out what the Expert report must contain:

> *(a) give details of the expert's qualifications, relevant experience and accreditation;*
>
> *(b) give details of any literature or other information which the expert has relied on in making the report;*
>
> *(c) contain a statement setting out the substance of all facts given to the expert which are material to the opinions expressed in the report, or upon which those opinions are based;*
>
> *(d) make clear which of the facts stated in the report are within the expert's own knowledge;*
>
> *(e) where the expert has based an opinion or inference on a representation of fact or opinion made by another person for the purposes of criminal proceedings (for example, as to the outcome of an examination, measurement, test or experiment)—*
>
> > *(i) identify the person who made that representation to the expert,*

(ii) give the qualifications, relevant experience and any accreditation of that person, and

(iii) certify that that person had personal knowledge of the matters stated in that representation;

(f) where there is a range of opinion on the matters dealt with in the report—

(i) summarise the range of opinion, and

(ii) give reasons for the expert's own opinion;

(g) if the expert is not able to give an opinion without qualification, state the qualification;

(h) include such information as the court may need to decide whether the expert's opinion is sufficiently reliable to be admissible as evidence;

(i) contain a summary of the conclusions reached;

(j) contain a statement that the expert understands an expert's duty to the court, and has complied and will continue to comply with that duty; and

(k) contain the same declaration of truth as a witness statement.

Failure to comply with the CrimPR does not render an Expert's Report or evidence automatically inadmissible. Where there has been a material failure to comply with the CrimPR by the Expert, the Court may refuse permission for the expert to be relied upon and/or (in the case of a Prosecution Expert) the Defence may apply for the exclusion of the expert's evidence under s78 Police and Criminal Evidence Act 1984:

> *In any proceedings the court may refuse to allow evidence on which the prosecution proposes to rely to be given if it appears to the court that, having regard to all the circumstances, including the circumstances in which the evidence was obtained, the admission of the evidence would have such an adverse effect on the fairness of the proceedings that the court ought not to admit it.*

In determining the admissibility of the Expert's evidence, the court is likely to consider; the extent of the failure to comply, any prejudice that has been caused, whether that prejudice can be remedied and whether, fundamentally, the expert is qualified to provide the opinion and is adhering to their overriding duty to the court.

6.2 Experts: Conflicts of Interest

Issues sometimes arise in s82 cases where it is alleged that the Expert has a conflict of interest. This is explicable when you consider the type of expert required for these cases. Environmental Health Practitioners tend to have the qualifications and experience to assess what does, and does not, amount to a statutory nuisance. These individuals gain their experience from working for Local Authorities and there is a relatively small pool who go on to provide Expert opinions.

This can create the perception of a conflict of interest for both Prosecution Experts and for Defence Experts.

The Prosecuting Firms tend to instruct Experts via an Agency on a fixed fee agreement. It has been known to happen that an Expert is employed by a company, or the Agency is a company, which is

connected to the Prosecuting Firm (eg. Through source of financing or company officers).

For Defence Experts the conflict of interest may be more obvious. The Defence are often Local Authorities, the Expert may previously have been employed by that Local Authority as an Environmental Health Officer or even continue to work on a freelance basis for that Local Authority as a contractor.

The Court of Appeal considered the issue of Expert conflicts of interest in the case of **Toth v Jarman [2006] EWCA Civ 1028**. The relevant parts of the Judgment are contained in paras 99-121, which set out the following principles:

1. A conflict of interest does not automatically disqualify an expert, the question is whether the conflict is material or significant and, fundamentally, whether the expert's opinion is independent;

2. The conflict of interest must be disclosed at the first reasonable opportunity, this will usually be at the point of service of the expert's report. Where the conflict arises later in proceedings, it should be disclosed as soon as reasonably practicable thereafter;

3. The opposing party should make any objection to the admission of the Expert as early as reasonably practicable;

4. It is not for the party calling the expert, or even both parties by agreement, to determine that the conflict is irrelevant, it is a matter for the court;

5. If the court determines that the conflict is material or significant and/or that it undermines the independence of the

expert's opinion, the court may refuse permission for that expert to be relied upon.

These principles are, to an extent, reflected in CrimPR Rule 19:

- CrimPR 19.2(3)(d) obliges all experts to disclose to the party instructing them anything (of which the expert is aware) that might reasonably be thought capable of undermining the expert's opinion or detracting from their credibility or impartiality.

- CrimPR r.19.3(3)(c): a party who wants to introduce expert evidence otherwise than as an admitted fact, must serve with the report notice of anything of which the party serving it is aware which might reasonably be thought be capable of undermining the reliability of the expert's opinion, or detracting from the credibility or impartiality of the expert.

- Unless the parties agree otherwise or the court directs, a party may not introduce expert evidence if that party has not complied with r.19.3(3)

6.3 Opposing Experts

If the Defence are seeking to rely on their own Expert, the Defence must serve their initial Expert Report in compliance with CrimPR Rule 19. Crim PR 19.6 then applies; the court will direct that there be a joint meeting of the experts, following which a joint report or summary of the points of agreement, points of dispute and reasons must be submitted to the court.

CrimPR Rule 19.6(4) provides:

> *A party may not introduce expert evidence without the court's permission if the expert has not complied with a direction under this rule.*

What this means is that, if the experts have not met and/or have not provided their joint report or summary, the court may refuse permission for one or both experts to be relied upon at all.

In s82 cases, it is better that the meeting between the experts begins with a joint inspection. The Defence expert will have inspected the property first (prior to the information being laid), the Prosecution expert is likely to have inspected the property much later (after the First Appearance and service of the Prosecution case). If the experts were simply to meet, the basis of information on which each expert relies is likely to be materially different. The nuisance may have developed or may have been, partially or wholly, abated in the intervening time.

The experts ought to observe the state of the premises at one time in the same conditions. That does not mean that their conclusions will be the same. For example, the experts may observe a collection of rodent droppings underneath a kitchen counter. One expert may conclude that some of the droppings are old (suggesting previous mice activity) but some are fresh (suggesting ongoing mice activity). The other expert may form the view that all of the droppings are old and that the absence of new droppings suggests that there is no ongoing activity. Their reasoning and the justifications for their different conclusions must be set out for the court to then determine the issue.

If the Prosecution are seeking an Abatement Order (s82(2)) at trial, it is strongly recommended that a further joint inspection takes place shortly before the trial so that both experts can provide the court with opinions on the state of the premises at that date (see Ch 4).

6.4 How the Court Assesses the Reliability of Expert Evidence

CrimPR PD7.1.2 lists factors which the court may take into account in determining the reliability of expert opinion.

In s82 cases with opposing experts, the court must assess which of the expert's opinions is to be preferred and will apply its own common sense in assessing which expert provides the more reliable opinion. To this end, it is essential that the expert's methodology is thorough, their observations are detailed and that the reasoning between those observations and their conclusions is clearly explained.

For example, the Prosecution expert notes that there is a gap around the pipework connecting the kitchen to the exterior wall and concludes that this gap is used as an ingress point for mice. The Defence expert notes the gap but concludes that it is not used as an ingress point. In assessing which of these opinions is to be preferred, the court will consider the detail of the observations which led the expert to that conclusion.

If the Prosecution expert has:

- measured the gap and it is over 5mm (the minimum size for a mouse to pass through),
- observed and photographed hairs and grease marks surrounding the hole (which suggest mice have passed through it);
- identified fresh mouse droppings in the surrounding area in the kitchen by observing their colour, appearance and feeling the droppings themselves to assess whether soft and new or hard and stale

their conclusion that this gap is an ingress point for mice is far more likely to be accepted by the court.

A bare opinion or one based on limited observation or reasoning, even from an appropriately qualified expert, is unlikely to be considered reliable.

CHAPTER SEVEN

DISCLOSURE

7.1 Disclosure: Primary, Secondary & Ongoing

S3 CPIA:

> *(1) The prosecutor must—*
>
> > *(a) disclose to the accused any prosecution material which has not previously been disclosed to the accused and which might reasonably be considered capable of undermining the case for the prosecution against the accused or of assisting the case for the accused , or*
> >
> > *(b) give to the accused a written statement that there is no material of a description mentioned in paragraph (a).*

By s7A of the same Act, if the Defence serve a Defence Statement the Prosecution must review disclosure in line with the above test and provide any further material which meets that test ("secondary disclosure").

The duty of disclosure is an ongoing duty. Whether or not a Defence Statement is served, the Prosecution are obliged to consider whether new material which comes into their possession meets the test or whether previously undisclosed material becomes disclosable because, for example, a new issue has been raised or further evidence has come to light.

7.1.1 Who has the obligation?

Issues often arise in s82 cases as the "prosecutor" is the Complainant. This means that any material which is in the Complainant's possession and came into their possession in connection with the case (s3(2)(a) CPIA) must be reviewed for the purposes of disclosure and, in any event, placed on the Schedule of Unused Material. The Prosecuting firm is an agent of the Complainant and so the same applies to material in their possession.

Prosecuting firms are advised to request that the Complainant provide them with all documentation they have (correspondence, photographs, messages, pest control reports etc) about the nuisance at the outset of proceedings so that they may conduct a proper review and prepare a Schedule of Unused Material. The Complainant should continue to provide all further material until the case concludes.

7.2 Disclosure & Legal Professional Privilege

In public prosecutions there is no relationship of client and lawyer existing between a witness and the Crown Prosecution Service ("CPS") (though there is such a relationship between the Police and the CPS) and so issues of Legal Professional Privilege ("LPP") versus disclosure rarely arise.

However, in s82 cases there is a relationship of client and lawyer between the Complainant and the Prosecuting Firm. This means that correspondence, conversations and documentation which pass between the Complainant and the Prosecuting firm:

a. for the purposes of legal advice; or

b. for the sole or dominant purpose of conducting existing or reasonably contemplated adversarial litigation;

are likely to be protected by LPP.

7.2.1 Disclosure v LPP: A Balancing Exercise?

Where documents are subject to LPP, that privilege is "the predominant public interest". It is not a matter of balancing the competing interests of disclosure against the Complainant's right to LPP.

In the case of **R v Derby Magistrates' Court, Ex p B [1995] 3 WLR 681** the House of Lords made clear that:

> *The principle that a client should be free to consult his legal advisers without fear of his communications being revealed [is] a fundamental condition on which the administration of justice as a whole rest[s]; that notwithstanding the public interest in securing that all relevant evidence [is] made available to the defence, legal professional privilege [is] to be upheld in all cases as the predominant public interest.*

As detailed in the Judgment of Lord Lloyd of Berwick (at p.17):

> *There may be circumstances in which the principle [of LPP] will work hardship on a third party seeking to assert his innocence. But in the overall interests of the administration of justice, it is better that the principle should be preserved in tact...the courts have for many years regarded legal professional privilege as the predominant public interest. A balancing exercise is not required in individual cases, because*

the balance must always come down in favour of upholding the privilege unless, of course, the privilege is waived."

7.2.2 Practical Considerations

The Prosecuting Firm should maintain a comprehensive Schedule of Sensitive Unused Material and should keep this under review for disclosure purposes (irrespective of LPP). Where an issue is raised as to whether a privileged document should be disclosed, often a statement from the prosecuting advocate that the document is subject to LPP and also that, irrespective of LPP, it has been reviewed and it does not meet the test for disclosure will be sufficient to deal with the issue.

A more difficult situation will arise where a document subject to LPP would otherwise be disclosable. As set out above, absent waiver of LPP, the document cannot be disclosed. The Prosecuting Firm should ask the Complainant whether they will expressly consent to waiver of LPP and provide them with advice as to the consequences.

If LPP is waived, the document should be disclosed. If LPP is not waived, the Prosecuting Firm may have to consider whether they can continue with the Prosecution without misleading the court. If they cannot, they would be obliged to withdraw. This would likely lead to the prosecution ultimately failing.

CHAPTER EIGHT

SENTENCING

8.1 The Terms of the Abatement Order

Under s82(2) where the court is satisfied that the nuisance exists or is likely to recur at the premises, *the court shall make an order for either or both of the following purposes:*

> *(a) requiring the defendant to abate the nuisance, within a time specified in the order, and to execute any works necessary for that purpose;*
>
> *(b) prohibiting a recurrence of the nuisance, and requiring the defendant within a time specified in the order, to execute any works necessary to prevent the recurrence*

If the court is satisfied that the nuisance exists, then the court shall make an order:

- requiring the defendant to abate the nuisance
- (and may also prohibit its recurrence)
- within a specified time; and
- to execute any works necessary for that purpose

If the court is satisfied that (although the nuisance is not presently in existence) the nuisance is likely to recur the court shall make an order:

- prohibiting its recurrence; and

- requiring the defendant to execute any works necessary to prevent recurrence

- within a specified time.

It must be understood that any failure to comply with an Abatement Order is a criminal offence contrary to s82(8). Clear and concise language must be used in the terms of the order. The order must be reasonably achievable; it must be possible to abate the nuisance/prevent its recurrence and carry out the necessary works within the time specified.

The format should follow the order set out above. Ie. for an abatement order for an ongoing nuisance, the order should begin by requiring the Defendant to abate the nuisance (and prohibit its recurrence), should then set the time period in which the Defendant must achieve this and specify the works necessary for this purpose.

The Prosecuting advocate should prepare a draft order prior to sentencing. Determining the proposed time period and the necessary works should be done in consultation with the Prosecution Expert. There should then be discussion between the parties as to the work which will be necessary and how long, realistically, it will take for the Defendant to execute those works.

As the order requires the Defendant to abate the nuisance, if they carry out all of the specified works and the nuisance remains at the end of the specified time, they will be in breach. It is therefore wise to include some additional time after the specified works can be completed in case further work is required to meet that purpose.

Inevitably the Complainant who will have lived with this nuisance for (most likely) an extended period of time will be keen that the nuisance is abated as soon as possible. The Prosecuting advocate must strike a

balance between ensuring that the order can reasonably be complied with on the one hand and ensuring that there is no an undue delay on the other.

The Court is not bound by the proposed terms of the order but is likely to be guided by the parties and the advice of the Expert(s).

8.2 Assessing Costs

By s82(12), where the court is satisfied that the nuisance was in existence at the date of complaint, the court shall order the Defendant:

- *in such proportions as appears fair and reasonable*
- *to pay the person bringing the proceedings such amount*
- *as the court considers reasonably sufficient to compensate him*
- *for any expenses properly incurred by him in the proceedings*

8.2.1 The Approach to Assessing Costs under s82(12)

The High Court recently considered how costs should be addressed (as well as other issues) in the case of **R (on the application of Parker) v Magistrates Court at Teeside [2022] EWHC 358 (Admin).**

This was an unusual s82 case in which the nuisance arose from the collapse of a party wall. Proceedings for an Abatement Order were successfully brought against both the freehold owner of the Complainant's property and the freehold owners of the neighbouring property. The nuisance was admitted by the Defendants and the terms of the Abatement Order were agreed. Costs were agreed with one of the Defendants and the issue for the court to determine was the quantum of costs to be paid by each remaining Defendant. The District Judge heard from the Defendants that they had no means to pay, refused to consider the Schedule of Costs which had been prepared by the Prosecution and ordered the Defendants to pay £100 on a joint and several basis.

Mr Justice Fordham considered all of the previous authorities on the issue of costs assessments under s82(12) (Paragraph 5 contains a useful precis of the preceding authorities) and gave the Judgment. At paragraph 20, he pointed out that there is a direct contrast between the usual prosecution costs provision in s18(1) Prosecution of Offences Act 1985 ("POOA") and the terms of s82(12). S18(1) POOA provides a discretion linked to a general formula. Whereas s82(12) is a duty involving a specific formula.

At paragraph 18, Mr Justice Fulham set out how that formula should be approached:

> *I think it would be helpful to gather together here some points of law which arise directly from the express language of that provision:*
>
> *(1) This is a statutory duty (the word is "shall"); not a discretion (as would be connoted by the word "may"). The duty, moreover, involves a specific formula. These features are significant. It is familiar in the law for courts to have conferred on them, by Parliament or by rules, general discretionary powers in relation to costs.*

(2) The discharge of the statutory duty involves the magistrates' court addressing three questions, all of which are set out in the statutory wording. They are:

- *Question 1. What "expenses" were "properly incurred" by the private prosecutor in the proceedings ("properly incurred expenses")? To illustrate this, any item or items of expenditure not "properly incurred" needs to be excluded.*

- *Question 2. What amount is "reasonably sufficient to compensate" the private prosecutor for the properly incurred expenses? To illustrate this, any amount which is higher than "reasonably sufficient to compensate" needs to be reduced to an amount which is "reasonably sufficient to compensate".*

- *Question 3. If there is more than one defendant responsible, what is a "fair and reasonable proportion" of the expenses identified by answering Questions 1 and 2 which any given defendant should be ordered to pay to the private prosecutor?*

(3) In Question 1, the question of propriety ("properly") is not freestanding. Propriety is about whether a step (the step involving the incurring of that item of costs) was a proper one for the private prosecutor to have taken ("properly incurred costs").

(4) In Question 2, the question of reasonableness ("reasonably") is not freestanding. Reasonableness goes to sufficiency, for a purpose: to compensate the private prosecutor ("reasonably sufficient to compensate").

> *(5) Questions 1-3 all engage an exercise of evaluative judgment – sometimes called "discretion" – to be performed by the magistrates' court. In Questions 1 and 2 the margin (or latitude) for evaluative judgment is reflected in the word "considers". In Question 3 it is reflected in the statutory word "appears". But the judgment (or discretion) arises in asking specific questions posed by the subsection. The magistrates' court thus has a latitude for evaluative judgment – including a judgment in identifying considerations which assist it or do not assist it – provided always that the magistrates' court asks the right questions, correctly recognises legal relevancies and irrelevancies, adopts an answer within the range of reasonable responses, and gives legally adequate reasons.*

At paragraph 25, Mr Justice Fulham concluded:

> *In my judgment, the District Judge clearly fell into error in his approach to the assessment of costs in the present case. If he had tracked the contours of this particular statutory provision, he would have found within it his 'route to verdict'. He would have asked the 3 Questions (§18(2)) embedded in the particular statutory language. He would have evaluated the contents of the costs schedule. He would have considered any "basis" on which it was "challenged" by the Interested Parties (see §8(ii) above). He would have addressed whether any items were to be excluded (as not "reasonably incurred expenses"); or whether any amounts were to be reduced as not "reasonably sufficient to compensate"); or whether there were any points regarding apportionment as between the Interested Parties or alongside ZCI (as a "fair and reasonable proportion"), in circumstances where ZCI's costs liability had been agreed (at £4,500). The District Judge did not – even in a broad brush, summary way – 'investigate' the position, in a way which set out to answer the 3 Questions, and which*

then enabled a reasoned conclusion by reference to those 3 Questions, so as to answer the main points which had been made.

8.2.2 The Questions for the Court to Answer

Assessing costs under s82(12) is a "broad brush" or "summary" process, nevertheless asking and answering the right questions involves some inquiry or investigation by the court to reach its evaluative answer (see para 22).

The questions to be asked and answered are:

1. What expenses were "properly incurred" by the Complainant? Propriety is about whether the step which incurred the costs was a proper one for the Prosecutor to have taken. If it was not, the item should be excluded.

2. What amount is "reasonably sufficient" to compensate for the "properly incurred" expenses? The question of reasonableness goes to the sufficiency of the compensation for that purpose, ie. whether the amounts claimed are more than is warranted, if so they should be reduced (see para 23).

3. If there is more than one Defendant, what is a "fair and reasonable proportion" of the expenses to order each Defendant to pay?

It should be noted that in most s82 cases there will be only one Defendant, in which case Question 3 does not need to be considered.

8.2.3 A Working Example

To give an example, the Costs Schedule includes 2 hours for a Grade A fee earner (at £398ph, total claimed is £796) to draft the Abatement Notice.

- Q1: Is this an expense which was "properly incurred"? Drafting the Abatement Order is a proper step to take (it is required by the Act).

- Q2: What amount is "reasonably sufficient" to compensate for this expense? The court may consider that 2 hours for a relatively simple notice is more time than was reasonably required. The court may also consider that this task did not need to be undertaken by a Grade A fee earner but could have been undertaken by a less qualified solicitor or legal executive (Grade C – £260ph). The amount should be duly reduced to a "reasonably sufficient" amount for the drafting of the Notice, eg. 1.5 hours Grade C – £390.

8.2.4 Practical Approach

Prosecuting advocates are all too ready to simply hand up the Costs Schedule to the court without reviewing it first. This is unhelpful and does not endear the costs application to the District Judge who will have to start the assessment from square one.

On receipt of the Costs Schedule, the advocate should go through the heads of expenses and address their minds to the questions set out above. The advocate should, in discussion with their instructing solicitor (if separate), go through each line of claim. Any repetition of work without good reason should be immediately cut out as the expense is not "properly incurred". Any other unnecessary or unjustifiable work should equally be cut. The advocate should then turn their mind to the amounts claimed on each remaining head; the time and the level of fee earner. Where work has been done by a Grade A fee earner (eg. Preparing the bundles for court) which really should have been done by a Grade D fee earner (trainee or paralegal), the hourly rate should be reduced. Where an apparently excessive amount of time has been spent on a task an explanation should be sought and, where there is no sufficient explanation, the time claimed should be reduced.

Once this has been done, the Prosecuting advocate should discuss the reduced Schedule of Costs with the Defence Advocate so that they may raise any issues with remaining amounts. If agreement can be reached, the Schedule can be further amended to reflect this. If agreement cannot be reached, it should be clear to both parties where issue is taken and the substance of that issue for the court to determine.

8.3 Fines & Compensation

The Court may only fine the Defendant and order them to pay compensation to the Complainant under s133-135 Sentencing Code 2020 (previously s35 Prosecution of Offences Act 1973) if the nuisance was in existence or likely to recur at the date of the hearing.

This is set out in the High Court Judgment in the case of **R v Dudley Magistrates' Court** [1999] 1 W.L.R. 642:

> *Section 82(2) creates a criminal offence in circumstances where a statutory nuisance exists at the time of the hearing or where, although abated, it is likely to recur ... Even if a statutory nuisance existed up to the day before the hearing, no offence has been committed, so long as the statutory nuisance*

is not likely to recur. Consequently, the court has no power to make any of the orders specified in that subsection, and, importantly, has no power to make an order of compensation pursuant to section 35 of the Powers of Criminal Courts Act 1973.

8.3.1 Fines

The Court may impose a fine up to Level 5 of the Standard Scale. Since March 2015, this is an unlimited amount (it was previously £5,000). There are no Sentencing Guidelines, which makes the court's assessment of the appropriate amount somewhat difficult. The Sentencing Guidelines: Overarching Principles should be considered and the court should be addressed on general 'Culpability' and 'Harm'.

In reality, the issue rarely arises. The Prosecutor should ask the court to give priority to compensation for the Complainant. This is the standard approach in criminal proceedings where there are issues as to the Defendant's means to pay both (see s135(4) Sentencing Code 2020). It is further endorsed by the case of **R v Liverpool Crown Court ex p Cooke** [1997] **1 WLR 700** in which the High Court stated that, where the compensation order was large enough to be punitive, a fine should not also be imposed.

In practice in s82 cases, this usually means that the court will order compensation but not a fine. There really is no need. There will be an Abatement Order which, if breached, would lead to a criminal conviction and a sentence of a maximum level 5 fine plus 10% of £5000 (£500) for each day the offence continues after conviction (s82(8)) and a costs order under s82(12).

The court may be persuaded to issue a fine as well as compensation where the Defendant is a "repeat offender", ie. where there have been multiple abatement orders made against the same defendant (in respect of different properties).

8.3.2 Compensation

A compensation order under s133 Sentencing Code 2020 requires the Defendant to pay the Complainant compensation for any personal injury, loss or damage resulting from the offence. The maximum amount which can be ordered by the Magistrates' Court is £5,000.

The Court may order compensation for distress and anxiety (**Bond v Chief Constable of Kent [1983] 1 All ER 456** and **Godfrey (1994) Crim App R** (s) 536). The order must take into account the means of the Defendant to pay the order within a reasonable time. Guidelines for compensating common injuries are set out in **The Magistrates' Court Sentencing Guidelines: Explanatory Materials: Compensation.**

The appropriate time period for the court to consider is from (at the earliest) the date of expiry of the Abatement Notice (see **R v Liverpool Crown Court ex p Cooke [1997] 1 WLR 700**).

If there has been a trial, the court will have heard from the Complainant as to the effect of the nuisance on themselves and their family. In some cases, there may be medical evidence, eg. If a child of the complainant has suffered from exacerbated asthma due to the mould. If there has been property damage (such as mould over furniture requiring it to be disposed of and replaced), as far as possible receipts should be produced for the costs of replacement.

Unlike the civil courts, the Magistrates Court will not conduct a detailed assessment of the appropriate figure for compensation. The general practice in s82 case varies, if the parties do not agree a figure for compensation the District Judge will usually come to a general figure taking into account the particularities of the case.

By experience, it can be seen that Judges take a multitude of factors into account. For example, if the Complainant is particularly vulnerable in some way, such as he or she has mental health issues which have been exacerbated by living in a property which was unsafe, that is likely to increase the figure. The presence of young children in a property infested with mice is likely to increase the figure. If the Defendant has been acting with all due expedience (even though the nuisance has not yet been abated) and pleaded Guilty at the first opportunity, that is likely to reduce the figure. If the Defendant has done nothing at all, this will work the opposite way. This may not be the typical practice in the general run of criminal cases, but it is the practice that tends to be adopted in s82 cases.

The parties may endeavour to agree the appropriate level of compensation and suggest that amount to the court, but the court is not bound by this. The court is often more inclined to interfere with an agreement as to the amount of compensation than they are to interfere with an agreement about costs or the terms of the Abatement Order. This may be due to the fact that the criminal courts are far more familiar with compensation orders than they are with Abatement Orders or Costs Orders.

CHAPTER NINE

SETTLING CASES

9.1 How to "Settle" a s82 Prosecution: What do you need to agree?

As set out at Ch 5.3, there are a limited number of ways in which a s82 prosecution comes to an end. Where the parties settle the case, it comes to an end when the Prosecution withdraws the summons.

The first point to consider when seeking to settle a case is which orders you would be seeking if you went to trial. This will give you the heads of agreement to be resolved.

If the nuisance is ongoing or likely to recur, you will need to agree:

1. The time in which the nuisance must be abated/prohibited from recurrence and the works to be done;

2. The amount to be paid to the Complainant as compensation under s133 Sentencing Code 2022;

3. The amount to be paid in costs;

4. The time by which those payments must be received.

If the nuisance has been abated but was present at the date of the information, you will need to agree the amount of costs only. The parties often also include a compensation payment to the Complainant even though this cannot be ordered by the court. This is of benefit to the Prosecution as the court cannot order compensation under these circumstances and will likely work to the benefit of the defence as the Prosecution may accept a lower amount in costs as a result.

9.2 Practical Considerations

The Summons should not be withdrawn until the settlement agreement has been fully executed. The matter should be adjourned for an agreed time period in which the parties believe that the terms of the settlement can be satisfied. If they are satisfied prior to the return date, the summons can be administratively withdrawn. If they are not, the Prosecution can continue.

Parties tend to use a "memorandum of agreement" for settlements in s82 cases. This is helpful as it is clear to both parties what must be done, what must be paid (and when) for the summons to then be withdrawn.

These are not civil proceedings, the memorandum of agreement will not become an enforceable court order. The court does not even need to see it, it is arguably covered by 'Without Prejudice Privilege'. The Court simply needs to be told that the parties have reached an agreement, the length of the adjournment sought for that agreement to be put into effect and the Prosecutor should confirm that the summons will be withdrawn once the agreement has been fully executed.

The memorandum should be clear enough that both parties know what must be done for the summons to be withdrawn. If the Prosecution proceed when the terms of the settlement have been satisfied the case would most likely be stayed as an abuse of the court's process by going back on a promise (see, eg **Mansfield v DPP [2021] EWHC 2938 (Admin)**, which also confirms that the Magistrates'

Court does have the power to stay proceedings in this category of abuse of process).

As a rule of thumb, in cases where otherwise an Abatement Order would be sought, the first term of the memorandum of agreement should be that the Defendant will abate the nuisance and/or prohibit its recurrence. This ensures that if all other agreed works are done, but for some reason these are ineffective, the prosecution remains extant until the nuisance is abated and its recurrence prohibited.

Do not withdraw the summons until the nuisance has been abated/its recurrence has been prohibited and costs (and compensation if any) have been paid. Once the summons has been withdrawn, even if the agreement is not then satisfied, the proceedings cannot be resurrected. The only option for the Prosecution will be to begin again with a new Abatement Notice. If, as may very well happen, the Defence have then managed to abate the nuisance by the date of the new information, the Prosecution will receive nothing.

CHAPTER TEN

CONDITIONAL FEE AGREEMENTS

10.1 Conditional Fee Agreements in Criminal Proceedings: The Sole Exception

By s58A(1) Courts and Legal Services Act 1990 ("CLSA") conditional fee agreements are prohibited in all criminal proceedings with one exception; proceedings under s82 EPA:

> *S58A – Conditional fee agreements: supplementary*
>
> *(1) The proceedings which cannot be the subject of an enforceable conditional fee agreement are—*
>
> > *(a) criminal proceedings, apart from proceedings under section 82 of the Environmental Protection Act 1990; and*
> >
> > *(b) family proceedings.*

10.2 Why the Exception?

This begs the question of why? Why are s82 EPA cases the sole exception to this prohibition? The answer is instructive to understanding the nature of these proceedings and the types of Complainants who tend to bring them. It is to be found in the legal context of two inconsistent decisions of the Court of Appeal and in the discussion which took place in Parliament as the cross-bench amendment was proposed and, initially, opposed by the Government.

S58 was replaced and s58A was inserted into the CLSA by the Access to Justice Act 1999, which took effect on 1st April 2000. At the time of its debate in the House of Commons, there had been two recent decisions of the Court of Appeal on the question of the enforceability of CFAs.

10.2.1 Two Court of Appeal Decisions: Thai Trading & Hughes v Kingston upon Hull

Thai Trading Co. (A Firm) v Taylor & Another [1998] 2 W.L.R. 893

This was a county court case. The Defendant had paid a deposit for a mattress, but then rejected it on delivery as unsatisfactory. The Claimant (then "plaintiff") made a claim for payment of the balance, the Defendant counterclaimed for return of the Deposit. The Defendant was represented by her solicitor husband on the basis that he would recover his ordinary profit costs if she succeeded and no fees if she did not. The claim was dismissed and the counterclaim succeeded. In the costs application, the Judge concluded that he was bound by authority to find that the arrangement was contrary to public policy and void as a contingency fee. As the Defendant was not liable to pay her own costs, by the indemnity principle, the Claimant was not liable to pay those costs.

The Court of Appeal held that the agreement was not contrary to public policy nor was it unlawful for the solicitor to act on a contingency fee basis provided he did not seek to recover more than his ordinary costs and disbursements if he won.

The Court of Appeal overruled the cases of and *Aratra Potato Co. Ltd. v. Taylor Joynson Garrett [1995] 4 All E.R. 695.*

Millett L.J. gave the judgment of the Court. Toward the end of that judgment, he sets out his reasoning:

> *I do not understand why it is assumed that the effect of the arrangement being unlawful is that the solicitor is unable to recover his proper costs in any circumstances. Where the solicitor contracts for a reward over and above his proper fees if he wins, it may well be that the whole retainer is unlawful and the solicitor can recover nothing. But where he contracts for no more than his proper fees if he wins, this result does not follow. There is nothing unlawful in the retainer or in the client's obligation to pay the solicitor's proper costs if he wins the case. If there is anything unlawful, it is in the waiver or reduction of the fees if he loses…*
>
> *… It is in my judgment fanciful to suppose that a solicitor will be tempted to compromise his professional integrity because he will be unable to recover his ordinary profit costs in a small case if the case is lost. Solicitors are accustomed to withstand far greater incentives to impropriety than this…*
>
> *Current attitudes to these questions are exemplified by the passage into law of the Courts and Legal Services Act 1990 . This shows that the fear that lawyers may be tempted by having a financial incentive in the outcome of litigation to act improperly is exaggerated, and that there is a countervailing public policy in making justice readily accessible to persons of modest means. Legislation was needed to authorise the increase in the lawyer's reward over and above his ordinary profit costs. It by no means follows that it was needed to legitimise the long-standing practice of solicitors*

to act for meritorious clients without means, and it is in the public interest that they should continue to do so.

This case was decided in February 1998; the Court of Appeal overruled the previous authorities suggesting that contingency fee agreements were unlawful and found that so-called "Thai Trading Agreements" (CFAs without an uplift or success fee) were lawful and consistent with the CLSA.

The next case came in November 1998: **Hughes v Kingston upon Hull City Council [1992] W.L.R 1229**

This was s82 EPA prosecution. The Complainant was an elderly impecunious pensioner who lived in a Council property affected by damp. She signed a retainer with the Prosecuting Firm which provided that it would recover its costs from the other side if the case was successful, but it was silent on the issue of costs in the event that the case failed. By the time of the trial, the nuisance had been abated and a costs order was sought under s82(12) EPA. The Stipendiary Magistrate found that the Prosecuting Firm were instructed on a contingency fee basis and that this was unenforceable as contrary to public policy, the proceedings being criminal in nature.

The Complainant appealed and this was dismissed by the Court of Appeal. The Court held that the Complainant could only recover costs that she was liable to pay, as there was no liability for her to pay the solicitors, no order for costs should be made. And, in any event, the agreement was a contingency fee agreement and therefore unenforceable.

Leave to appeal was refused at the hearing. But, interestingly, on 25th

March 1999 the Court of Appeal certified under s1(2) of the Administration of Justice Act 1960 that the following point of law of general public importance was involved in the decision, namely: *"Are speculative fee agreements lawful, in particular in criminal cases where the solicitor claims costs from the other side if he wins and where there is no intention to create any liability for their own costs if proceedings fail?"*

Ultimately that question never went to the Supreme Court, it was answered by Primary Legislation.

10.2.2 The Amendment in Parliament

This brings us squarely to the discussion in Parliament over the amendment to s58A(1)(a) to exclude s82 EPA prosecutions from the prohibition on CFAs in criminal cases.

To put it into context this was at a point when Legal Aid had recently been significantly restricted and was, in any event, not available to Complainants in Criminal cases. The amendment was a cross-bench amendment, supported by the Law Society and (importantly) by the charity Shelter. It was initially opposed by the Government who were against providing a singular exception to the prohibition on CFAs in criminal (and family) proceedings. Over the course of multiple debates, the Government eventually conceded, the amendment passed and was then enacted in April 2000.

As can be seen upon reading the debates, the express intention of s58 and s58A was to place the **Thai Trading** decision onto statutory footing. The amendment was to overrule **Hughes v Kingston upon Hull** to ensure that CFAs could be used in s82 cases.

The argument, sometimes advanced by the Defence in these cases, that the court cannot order costs under a CFA in a s82(12) Costs Order as they are not costs "properly incurred" by the Complainant and/or are not costs to "compensate" the Complainant is wrong. The amendment to s58A(1)(a) is expressly intended to ensure that the Court can order costs to be paid to the Complainant's instructed solicitors under a CFA in a s82 prosecution.

In the course of the Debates, on Tuesday 22nd June 1999, Nick Hawkins (barrister and Conservative MP for Surrey Heath) argued strongly for the amendment:

> *Unless the amendment is accepted, Parliament will give people a right to take action in respect of housing disrepair and certain other nuisances even though it intends to deny those affected the means to enforce their rights.*
>
> *Sadly, tenants of houses in disrepair are, by definition, likely to be of limited means… it is extremely rare for such tenants to have the means to fund the legal cost of taking enforcement action. Magistrates court proceedings are an effective means of securing a remedy in such cases. The Law Society rightly says that tenants usually rely on solicitors being willing to take a case in the knowledge that, if unsuccessful, the tenant will be unable to pay their costs…*
>
> *[Without the amendment] the rights given to tenants under section 82 of the Environmental Protection Act 1990 by the last Government would become meaningless. The Bill is called the Access to Justice Bill, but, as the Law Society rightly says, there will be no access to justice for such tenants if it is left unamended.*

10.3 Why does it matter?

The permissibility of CFAs by s58A(1)(a) CLSA is fundamental to the effective operation of the tenants' right to redress under s82. CFAs are not a side issue. Without CFAs, s82 would essentially exist in name only.

The question, which it appears finally forced the government to rethink its opposition, was posed by Gareth Thomas (Labour MP for Harrow West):

> *I understand the argument that my hon. Friend the Minister is making, but perhaps I could press him on one matter. How does he anticipate that those rather important cases brought under the Environmental Protection Act 1990 will be financed in future?*

Humfrey Mallins (Barrister, Crown Court Recorder, Deputy District Judge and Conservative MP for Woking) made a speech in the House of Commons on Wednesday 21st July 1999, as the amendment passed;

> *The concept of the tenant being unable to receive legal help with complaints against a bad landlord is one with which no Member of the House should be happy. The ability for us to say that conditional fee agreements should apply to proceedings under section 82 of the Environmental Protection Act is a major step forward. It is more significant than many hon. Members appreciate, because it takes a huge step towards enabling tenants to obtain justice. As my hon. Friend the Member for Surrey Heath said, Shelter has supported that proposition throughout.*

You may, unfortunately, encounter in the Criminal Courts some reluctance to make costs orders under s82(12) in cases funded by a CFA. You may find there is some cynicism on behalf of the court and the Defence about the use of these funding arrangements and the Prosecuting Firm's objectives. The Criminal Courts are not used to CFAs which may provide some explanation for this.

But the accusation that Prosecuting Firms funded by CFAs are somehow acting in an underhand manner motived by improper purposes is wrong. If it were not for these firms, s82 would effectively not exist. The most vulnerable tenants, who require redress to the Criminal Courts where their landlords have failed (often repeatedly) to make their homes safe for them, can only access that redress because of firms willing to take the risk and fund the matter by a CFA.

Far from the (oft made) suggestion that these firms will pursue unmeritorious claims, the effect of CFA funding is the opposite. Prosecuting firms instructed under CFAs conduct careful assessments of each case prior to issue (and ongoing) to limit the risk that hours may be spent, and disbursements paid, only for the firm to then suffer the loss.

The other (oft made) suggestion that Prosecuting Firms profit illegitimately from CFAs is also wrong. They recover only the time spent on proper tasks to advance the case at the rates that the court consider to be sufficient.

10.4 Practical Considerations: Success Fees & Legal Professional Privilege

By s2 Conditional Fee Agreements Order 2013, a CFA for a s82 case cannot include a success fee (nor any other uplift). If a prosecution is successful, the Complainant may only seek the costs of the time actually spent by the Prosecuting Firm on the case and their disbursements (Counsel's fees are usually paid as a disbursement as opposed to Counsel also taking on the CFA). This ties in with the logic set out above of s58A(1)(a) placing *"Thai Trading Agreements"* onto statutory footing for EPA cases.

It should be noted that the CFA itself is covered by LPP. Where an issue is raised by the Defence, as it often is, about the CFA the Prosecuting Advocate should seek a copy of the written agreement and review it. Once satisfied that it is a lawful CFA (ie. there is no success fee or other uplift), this can be confirmed to the court and the document would not be disclosable as it would neither assist the defence nor undermine the prosecution, irrespective of privilege.

The Court ought to have in mind the Prosecuting Advocate's duty not to mislead as well as the paramountcy of privilege, and that ought to be the end of the matter. Sometimes it is not, some courts have refused to make s82(12) costs orders in CFA funded cases, citing different reasons and justifications. There has yet to be a case where this is tested in the higher courts. It is understood that one may be pending.

MORE BOOKS BY LAW BRIEF PUBLISHING

'A Practical Guide to Confiscation and Restraint' by Narita Bahra QC, John Carl Townsend, David Winch
'A Practical Guide to the Law of Forests in Scotland' by Philip Buchan
'A Practical Guide to Health and Medical Cases in Immigration Law' by Rebecca Chapman & Miranda Butler
'A Practical Guide to Bad Character Evidence for Criminal Practitioners by Aparna Rao
'A Practical Guide to Extradition Law post-Brexit' by Myles Grandison et al
'A Practical Guide to Hoarding and Mental Health for Housing Lawyers' by Rachel Coyle
'A Practical Guide to Psychiatric Claims in Personal Injury – 2nd Edition' by Liam Ryan
'Stephens on Contractual Indemnities' by Richard Stephens
'A Practical Guide to the EU Succession Regulation' by Richard Frimston
'A Practical Guide to Solicitor and Client Costs – 2nd Edition' by Robin Dunne
'Constructive Dismissal – Practice Pointers and Principles' by Benjimin Burgher
'A Practical Guide to Religion and Belief Discrimination Claims in the Workplace' by Kashif Ali
'A Practical Guide to the Law of Medical Treatment Decisions' by Ben Troke
'Fundamental Dishonesty and QOCS in Personal Injury Proceedings: Law and Practice' by Jake Rowley
'A Practical Guide to the Law in Relation to School Exclusions' by Charlotte Hadfield & Alice de Coverley
'A Practical Guide to Divorce for the Silver Separators' by Karin Walker
'The Right to be Forgotten – The Law and Practical Issues' by Melissa Stock
'A Practical Guide to Planning Law and Rights of Way in National Parks, the Broads and AONBs' by James Maurici QC, James Neill et al
'A Practical Guide to Election Law' by Tom Tabori
'A Practical Guide to the Law in Relation to Surrogacy' by Andrew Powell
'A Practical Guide to Claims Arising from Fatal Accidents – 2nd Edition' by James Patience
'A Practical Guide to the Ownership of Employee Inventions – From Entitlement to Compensation' by James Tumbridge & Ashley Roughton
'A Practical Guide to Asbestos Claims' by Jonathan Owen & Gareth McAloon

'A Practical Guide to Stamp Duty Land Tax in England and Northern Ireland' by Suzanne O'Hara
'A Practical Guide to the Law of Farming Partnerships' by Philip Whitcomb
'Covid-19, Homeworking and the Law – The Essential Guide to Employment and GDPR Issues' by Forbes Solicitors
'Covid-19 and Criminal Law – The Essential Guide' by Ramya Nagesh
'Covid-19 and Family Law in England and Wales – The Essential Guide' by Safda Mahmood
'A Practical Guide to the Law of Unlawful Eviction and Harassment – 2nd Edition' by Stephanie Lovegrove
'Covid-19, Brexit and the Law of Commercial Leases – The Essential Guide' by Mark Shelton
'A Practical Guide to Costs in Personal Injury Claims – 2nd Edition' by Matthew Hoe
'A Practical Guide to the General Data Protection Regulation (GDPR) – 2nd Edition' by Keith Markham
'Ellis on Credit Hire – Sixth Edition' by Aidan Ellis & Tim Kevan
'A Practical Guide to Working with Litigants in Person and McKenzie Friends in Family Cases' by Stuart Barlow
'Protecting Unregistered Brands: A Practical Guide to the Law of Passing Off' by Lorna Brazell
'A Practical Guide to Secondary Liability and Joint Enterprise Post-Jogee' by Joanne Cecil & James Mehigan
'A Practical Guide to the Pre-Action RTA Claims Protocol for Personal Injury Lawyers' by Antonia Ford
'A Practical Guide to Neighbour Disputes and the Law' by Alexander Walsh
'A Practical Guide to Forfeiture of Leases' by Mark Shelton
'A Practical Guide to Coercive Control for Legal Practitioners and Victims' by Rachel Horman
'A Practical Guide to the Law of Driverless Cars – Second Edition' by Alex Glassbrook, Emma Northey & Scarlett Milligan
'A Practical Guide to TOLATA Claims' by Greg Williams
'A Practical Guide to Elderly Law – 2nd Edition' by Justin Patten
'A Practical Guide to Responding to Housing Disrepair and Unfitness Claims' by Iain Wightwick

‘A Practical Guide to the Law of Bullying and Harassment in the Workplace’ by Philip Hyland
‘How to Be a Freelance Solicitor: A Practical Guide to the SRA-Regulated Freelance Solicitor Model’ by Paul Bennett
‘A Practical Guide to Prison Injury Claims’ by Malcolm Johnson
‘A Practical Guide to the Small Claims Track – 2nd Edition’ by Dominic Bright
‘A Practical Guide to Advising Clients at the Police Station’ by Colin Stephen McKeown-Beaumont
‘A Practical Guide to Antisocial Behaviour Injunctions’ by Iain Wightwick
‘Practical Mediation: A Guide for Mediators, Advocates, Advisers, Lawyers, and Students in Civil, Commercial, Business, Property, Workplace, and Employment Cases’ by Jonathan Dingle with John Sephton
‘The Mini-Pupillage Workbook’ by David Boyle
‘A Practical Guide to Crofting Law’ by Brian Inkster
‘A Practical Guide to the Law of Domain Names and Cybersquatting’ by Andrew Clemson
‘A Practical Guide to the Law of Gender Pay Gap Reporting’ by Harini Iyengar
‘NHS Whistleblowing and the Law’ by Joseph England
‘Employment Law and the Gig Economy’ by Nigel Mackay & Annie Powell
‘A Practical Guide to Noise Induced Hearing Loss (NIHL) Claims’ by Andrew Mckie, Ian Skeate, Gareth McAloon
‘An Introduction to Beauty Negligence Claims – A Practical Guide for the Personal Injury Practitioner’ by Greg Almond
‘Intercompany Agreements for Transfer Pricing Compliance’ by Paul Sutton
‘Zen and the Art of Mediation’ by Martin Plowman
‘A Practical Guide to the SRA Principles, Individual and Law Firm Codes of Conduct 2019 – What Every Law Firm Needs to Know’ by Paul Bennett
‘A Practical Guide to Adoption for Family Lawyers’ by Graham Pegg
‘A Practical Guide to Industrial Disease Claims’ by Andrew Mckie & Ian Skeate
‘A Practical Guide to Conducting a Sheriff Court Proof’ by Andrew Stevenson
‘A Practical Guide to Vicarious Liability’ by Mariel Irvine
‘A Practical Guide to Applications for Landlord’s Consent and Variation of Leases’ by Mark Shelton
‘A Practical Guide to Relief from Sanctions Post-Mitchell and Denton’ by Peter Causton

'A Practical Guide to Equity Release for Advisors' by Paul Sams
'A Practical Guide to Financial Services Claims' by Chris Hegarty
'The Law of Houses in Multiple Occupation: A Practical Guide to HMO Proceedings' by Julian Hunt
'Occupiers, Highways and Defective Premises Claims: A Practical Guide Post-Jackson – 2nd Edition' by Andrew Mckie
'A Practical Guide to Financial Ombudsman Service Claims' by Adam Temple & Robert Scrivenor
'A Practical Guide to Running Housing Disrepair and Cavity Wall Claims: 2nd Edition' by Andrew Mckie & Ian Skeate
'A Practical Guide to Holiday Sickness Claims – 2nd Edition' by Andrew Mckie & Ian Skeate
'Arguments and Tactics for Personal Injury and Clinical Negligence Claims' by Dorian Williams
'A Practical Guide to Drone Law' by Rufus Ballaster, Andrew Firman, Eleanor Clot
'A Practical Guide to Compliance for Personal Injury Firms Working With Claims Management Companies' by Paul Bennett
'RTA Allegations of Fraud in a Post-Jackson Era: The Handbook – 2nd Edition' by Andrew Mckie
'RTA Personal Injury Claims: A Practical Guide Post-Jackson' by Andrew Mckie
'On Experts: CPR35 for Lawyers and Experts' by David Boyle
'An Introduction to Personal Injury Law' by David Boyle

These books and more are available to order online direct from the publisher at www.lawbriefpublishing.com, where you can also read free sample chapters. For any queries, contact us on 0844 587 2383 or mail@lawbriefpublishing.com.

Our books are also usually in stock at www.amazon.co.uk with free next day delivery for Prime members, and at good legal bookshops such as Wildy & Sons.

We are regularly launching new books in our series of practical day-to-day practitioners' guides. Visit our website and join our free newsletter to be kept informed and to receive special offers, free chapters, etc.

You can also follow us on Twitter at www.twitter.com/lawbriefpub.

www.ingramcontent.com/pod-product-compliance
Ingram Content Group UK Ltd.
Pitfield, Milton Keynes, MK11 3LW, UK
UKHW020150290926
15471UKWH00004B/787

9 781916 698055